CANAL ARCHITECTURE IN BRITAIN

An introduction to the fascinating buildings and structures of our waterways

FOREWORD

by Sir Frank Price DL FSVA FCIT ***Chairman of the British Waterways Board***

opposite: The flight of eight Delph Locks on the Dudley Canal near Brierley Hill, Birmingham

this page: The lock house at Hampstead Road, Camden Town, on the Regent's Canal, recently renovated and extended by the Board

The purpose of this publication is to draw attention to the many attractive buildings, which we consider worthy of conservation, still remaining alongside our waterways. Skilled treatment is needed to retain their historic character, while making sure they are not museum pieces but working elements of a living system.

The Board are the custodians of a number of listed buildings. Some of their properties are already part of conservation areas and some waterways restoration schemes have received the distinction of Civic Trust awards. The pace of canal rehabilitation has increased in the last few years and is likely to continue, thanks to local authority and voluntary help. Restoration schemes have included the repair of a number of waterside buildings, and the Board have a programme of renovating a small number of maintenance yards, buildings and structures each year. After long years of neglect, the waterways are now in the custody of people who care. Time and nature have made their mark; the dilapidations of a century cannot be made good in a few years, and the Board's resources are inadequate for their tasks.

The architectural heritage of the waterways consists not only of the features which can be identified, named and illustrated but of the system as a whole, a 19th century creation which has survived into the 20th to serve new purposes of commerce, recreation and aesthetic pleasure. The waterway builders constructed lasting monuments to their skill, a heritage which is worth preserving.

European Architectural Heritage Year 1975 made many more people aware of the richness of Europe's unique architecture. During the year the Board received a special award for continuing contributions to conservation and awards for their schemes in Cheshire, West Yorkshire and Greater Manchester. The Year has taught people to look at familiar buildings and structures with a new interest and a greater appreciation. More funds, however, must be forthcoming if the Board are to continue to foster the developing affection among groups and individuals for our splendid canalside buildings.

CONTENTS

opposite: The flight of locks and toll house at Bratch, near Wolverhampton, on the Staffordshire & Worcestershire Canal

this page: The lock cottage at Cowroast near Tring on the Grand Union Canal

CALEDONIAN
CRINAN
FORTH & CLYDE, MONKLAND, UNION
LANCASTER
LEEDS & LIVERPOOL
AIRE & CALDER NAVIGATION
HUDDERSFIELD NARROW
SHEFFIELD & S. YORKSHIRE
PEAK FOREST, MACCLESFIELD
TRENT NAVIGATION
FOSSDYKE & WITHAM NAVIGATIONS
LLANGOLLEN BRANCH
TRENT & MERSEY
SHROPSHIRE UNION
COVENTRY, ASHBY
MONTGOMERY BRANCH
B.C.N.
STAFFS. & WORCESTER
GRAND UNION
WORCESTER & BIRMINGHAM
SEVERN, GLOS. & SHARPNESS
MONMOUTHSHIRE & BRECON
GRAND UNION
SOUTH OXFORD
LEE NAVIGATION
KENNET & AVON
BRIDGWATER & TAUNTON
REGENT'S CANAL
Lune Aqueduct
Bingley Five Rise
Banavie
Lincoln Cathedral
Braunston Junction
Lift Bridge
Newbury Bridge

THE CANAL BUILDERS

When canals were built they must have been scars on the landscape as hideous as any motorway construction site. Nowadays, by skilful landscaping, a motorway is made to merge with the surrounding countryside as unobtrusively as possible.

No such remedy was available in the 18th and 19th centuries. Contemporary accounts complained that newly completed canal workings were a continuous sea of mud; others described the hard-edged white towing path running as far as the eye could see.

Nature has had two hundred years or so to perform the task of landscaping contractor and the job has been admirably done. The canalside is green, with plants fringing the water and wild roses in summer enhancing the towing path hedge, planted to mark the canal company's boundary. Buildings and structures have weathered and blended. Beautified by time, the canals evoke the nostalgia of a past industrial age – a nostalgia which is leading many people to re-examine the architectural contribution of Britain's great early engineers.

Because so many of its features have remained intact, canal architecture illustrates the progress of civil engineering from the late 18th century onwards. It provides a unique opportunity to study the progression from basic early techniques to the later sophistication of Rennie and Telford. Most 18th century canal building was purely functional, with little concern for ostentation. This produced a pleasing simplicity characteristic of the time, dictated by commercial demands and often by lack of funds. Subsequent examples show the influence of early 19th century classicism, or Victorian industrial gothic, and have a more ornamental appearance. It was seldom, however, that buildings or structures were conceived with an obviously decorative purpose.

this page: A typical bridge keeper's house of the Gloucester & Sharpness Ship Canal

The canal systems of England, Wales and Scotland were largely created during the late 18th and early 19th centuries. Previous schemes had concentrated on canalisation (or improving rivers for navigation) but the

A canalside pottery in Stoke-on-Trent

The Star Inn at Stone on the Trent & Mersey Canal

The ornamental Avenue Bridge on the Shropshire Union Canal near Wheaton Aston

canal age really began with the opening of the Duke of Bridgewater's Canal near Manchester in 1761.

This, a private venture, was followed by the formation of canal companies. Some built the canals which exist today, and some speculated on more far-fetched ideas which were never undertaken. Men like Josiah Wedgwood, who promoted the Trent & Mersey Canal, and Charles Dundas, who was actively involved in the construction of the Kennet & Avon Canal, rightly saw the waterways as the arteries of a new commercial age. Water transport enabled coal to be taken to communities which before had only charcoal, so that more efficient coal-based industries could be developed alongside the system which fed them with raw materials and took away their finished products.

It seems that the Bridgewater Canal was put together by the Duke himself, by his agent John Gilbert and by James Brindley – a millwright who became one of the first great civil engineers. Most canal companies engaged an eminent engineer of the day to give his views on a project, and then employed a resident engineer to design and supervise the new construction. Imposing canal company headquarters and structures such as tunnels, embankments and aqueducts were frequently designed by the resident engineer but with certain exceptions ordinary buildings such as warehouses, workshops, toll offices and canal cottages were produced to a generalised specification by the contractor in the simple manner of the period and locality.

At the time of canal construction, the new channel inevitably interrupted existing roads, tracks and field paths; to maintain the continuity of these routes, bridges of various sizes had to be provided. Most often found are the hump-backed accommodation bridges, needed by a farmer to move his livestock from one side of the navigation to the other. In brick or stone, they were all individually made and are never quite identical in appearance. In addition, cheaper moveable structures were made to swing up or sideways to allow boats to pass along the canal. Bridges carrying the approach road to a stately home were often ornamented at the request of the inhabitant, while some highway bridges, because of the volume of traffic, were constructed more solidly. Aqueducts were needed to carry the canal across rivers, streams and roads. Early ones were made of stone or brick, massively built although sometimes delightfully delicate in appearance; as engineering confidence increased they achieved soaring proportions and often consisted of much lighter cast iron troughs supported on masonry pillars.

The standard type of British canal lock, known as the pound lock, was the key to the transport revolution which opened communications across the centre of the country. Locks enabled a canal, by changing its level, to penetrate into undulating countryside and to cross a watershed in order to join one navigable river to another, thus linking towns, markets and coastal outlets. All possess interesting design features and there are unusual examples, for instance the diamond-shaped weir locks where the River Cherwell flows into the Oxford Canal. Variations exist in the use of materials such as turf, timber, brick or stone for the lock chamber walls. The footbridges provided for the person who is operating the lock show a fascinating diversity, from the Caldon Canal, where a wrought-iron cantilevered support is provided, to the Stratford-upon-Avon Canal split bridges whose twin halves are iron brackets cantilevered out from a brick abutment on each side. Lockside paddles and bollards, together with the textures of paved and cobbled horse ramps, steps and surfacing add up to a coherent working environment. Wear and tear seen in grooved bollards and depressions in steps create an emotional response in the observer who reflects on the constant use of these objects in the canals' commercial heyday.

At locks and waterway junctions, the focal points of activity, canal companies constructed buildings to accommodate toll clerks, lock keepers and maintenance staff, workmen, horses, pumping engines, stored material – and even catered for the boatmen's thirst by providing waterside pubs. Factories and warehouses, belonging to the canal company or to private commercial concerns, were intimately associated with the canal. Wharves allowed for the movement of goods to and from the waiting boats, while crane hoists jutting out over the water made speedy loading possible beneath. A number of examples still exist. Although, sadly, they are often derelict now, industry having gravitated to the roads, they can be restored and given new functions.

Canal construction was carried out by the crudest methods, the only tools employed being the pick, shovel and wheelbarrow, and the strength of a navvy's limbs. Respect is therefore due to the early builders who, without the benefit of modern methods of measurement and construction, created a system which is largely still serviceable and often well used. There is an immense variety of structures, resulting from regional differences, special requirements and the individual approach of each canal company. The chapters which follow attempt to identify and explain the trends resulting in such a wealth of architectural interest.

The Board's maintenance yard at Burscough on the Leeds & Liverpool Canal near Wigan

The lock cottage at Cropredy on the south Oxford Canal

The Bridge Inn at Ratho, Lothian, on the Union Canal in Scotland

FIRST PRINCIPLES

Britain's canals were created to remedy a state of affairs where it was more practical to import goods or carry them round the coast from one port to another than to send them across country, because of the appalling state of the roads. Narrow horse-tracks in summer which became sunken potholed ditches in winter, the roads of the 18th century would not permit any large-scale transport of goods. Rivers canalised in the 17th and 18th centuries did enable commodities to be taken to some inland destinations. The canals, a revolutionary form of transport, facilitated the change from a predominantly agricultural society to one based on manufacture. They fed the mills with raw materials and encouraged the expansion of trade by taking their products away to be sold.

Many architects today see functionalism as a shining light, in reaction to the decorated and imitative work of the Victorians. The early canal builders were unconscious disciples of the functional tradition, and the forms they created were suited to their purpose because that was all that mattered. The buildings associated with this phase were simple and unaffected. An accommodation bridge was not conceived as a graceful arch, but as a device using small-scale units (burnt clay bricks or stone) to link one field to its neighbour beyond the canal. It had to be strong, to bear cows and carts; it had to be small and inexpensive. That something of simple beauty was created was no doubt a source of satisfaction to the contractor, but it was scarcely among his objectives.

The first phase of canal engineering, in the 18th century, was characterised by a cautious approach, revealed especially in a reluctance to build costly items such as locks, embankments and aqueducts. Long flights of locks needed an ample and reliable water supply. Thus canals such as Brindley's Trent & Mersey, Staffordshire & Worcestershire and south Oxford, and Smeaton's Calder & Hebble and Scottish Forth & Clyde, cling to the contours of the land, avoiding abrupt changes in level. They meander through the countryside following a course not unlike that of a natural river and create an impression of unhurried calm. The long pounds between locks act as extra reservoirs to conserve precious water.

opposite: The south Oxford Canal at Napton in the Midlands

The Bridgewater canal had 'wide' locks (capable of accommodating one broad canal boat) but Brindley decided in favour of a narrower 7ft gauge for his other

The aqueduct over the river Goyt at Marple near Stockport in Cheshire, carrying the Peak Forest Canal

The bridge at Cropredy on the South Oxford Canal

The roving bridge at Marple, Cheshire, over the Macclesfield Canal at its junction with the Peak Forest Canal

A typical simple curved brick bridge on the Oxford Canal

canals, with locks which could only take one narrow boat at a time and were much less demanding on the water supply. The 'narrow' canals are not a uniform 7ft width throughout their length – of course they widen out between locks and bridges for boats to moor and pass – but their small dimensions add to the sense of intimacy and secrecy which characterises many fascinating urban waterside areas.

There is a certain endearing naivety in the accommodation bridges and lock cottages of this early phase. Traditional construction methods, together with local materials, gave each canal and region its own particular flavour. Mellow red brick was one of the commonest materials to be used in the Midlands, where good building stone was scarce, lending a warmth of tone to many industrial surroundings and acquiring a sculptural interest in the simple shapes of the pottery kilns around Stoke-on-Trent. In Birmingham red brick is often complemented by the decorative cast-iron bridges of the 19th century engineers. At Cropredy, on the Oxford Canal, blue engineering brick was used to trim the lines of a bridge which, having been built to take a road, is more substantial in construction than diminutive red brick accommodation bridges. It was common for a brickworks to be set up near to the site of canal construction, bricks being made of clay from the workings.

Structures were thus created from the materials through which the canal was dug. On the Staffordshire & Worcestershire, Peak Forest, Leeds & Liverpool and Monmouthshire & Brecon Canals, local stone obtained when the channel was made creates a rugged effect, giving dignity to buildings, bridges and aqueducts. The "snake" bridge at Marple, for example, spans the junction of the Macclesfield and Peak Forest Canals, and is designed to enable a horse to cross it without the towing rope having to be unhitched. This is a splendid example of stone being shaped into graceful lines with unconscious artistry. The very early aqueducts were dumpy like Brindley's River Sow aqueduct near Great Haywood on the Staffordshire & Worcestershire Canal. Their heavy construction precluded any great height being reached, in contrast to Benjamin Outram's magnificent aqueduct crossing the Goyt Valley at Marple. Here, at the springing point of each arched abutment, are pierced apertures to reduce the dead weight bearing on the piers. The features essential to the construction are trimmed in brick, giving an unintentional decorative effect which was later copied elsewhere as a form of ornamentation. Similar, although even grander in scale, are the Almond and Avon aqueducts on the Union Canal in Scotland.

Deep cuttings were a monumental task for the 18th century engineers. They preferred constructing tunnels, which posed fewer problems in slipping of the sides and the amount of spoil to be dug out. They were made by sinking a series of shafts, down which men and materials could be lowered. The shafts were then linked underground and subsequently used for ventilation. The portals had scant ornamentation, and one thinks of Brindley's original Harecastle tunnel at Kidsgrove on the Trent & Mersey Canal which like most early tunnels had no towpath, but a horse-track over the top of the hill. The boats were *legged* through. Later tunnels were given towing paths. Some early tunnels were later opened out into cuttings, such as at Fenny Compton on the south Oxford Canal, and at Armitage on the Trent & Mersey.

The early canal builders had no conception of involving architects in the design of lock cottages and other workers' dwellings. So a simple, rural domestic plan was adopted, with a steeply pitched roof and casement windows often surmounted by segmental arches. Some lock cottages have a special side window giving a view along the canal so that the lock-keeper could see when boats were approaching. One could point to hundreds of locations where this description fits exactly,

above: Stourport, where the Staffordshire & Worcestershire Canal meets the River Severn, with the Tontine Hotel in the centre

left: The northern entrance to Harecastle Tunnel on the Trent & Mersey Canal

The lock cottage at Tixall near Stafford on the Staffordshire & Worcestershire Canal

Fradley Junction, near Lichfield, where the Coventry and Trent & Mersey Canals meet

Cottages at Stourport

but Tixall (Staffordshire & Worcestershire Canal), Tardebigge (Worcester & Birmingham Canal) and Somerton (Oxford Canal) are good examples. Other buildings of the period, such as canalside pubs, are bigger versions of this canal vernacular. The grouping of lockside cottage and bridge is a classic ingredient of the visual canal experience.

The trade generated by the navigation gave rise to buildings orientated towards the water. Where the canal passed near to existing villages, such as Braunston, they developed a new quarter associated with the waterway and its industry: cottages, workshops, stables, stores and pubs. Some, like Stoke Bruerne on William Jessop's Grand Junction Canal (now part of the Grand Union), or Burnley on the Leeds & Liverpool, were bisected by the canal. Others, such as Hawkesbury where the Coventry and Oxford Canals meet, bore little relationship to existing settlements but arose from the needs of a canal junction or terminus. The 18th century contour canals often passed villages at a distance to avoid many changes of level en route. This led to the establishment of wharf areas away from the village they served. Hanbury Wharf, for instance, on the Worcester & Birmingham Canal near Droitwich, is not close to Hanbury itself. Fradley (Trent & Mersey and Coventry Canals) acquired workshops, stables, cottages and a waterside pub, creating a community isolated both in distance and by livelihood from the village of that name. House building at the turn of the 18th century in towns like Birmingham was stimulated in areas where canals had been constructed; soon they were occupied by people who would work in the new mills and factories served by water transport.

In some instances whole towns sprang up, the most notable being Stourport, where the Staffordshire & Worcestershire Canal joins the River Severn. Built under the guidance of James Brindley, this canal town still contains many features of the late 18th century and is much visited because of its extensive boat basins and attractive buildings. The cottages by the broad lock are listed as being of architectural and historical interest and Wyre Forest District Council received a special Heritage Year grant for a landscaping scheme at the basins. Aspects of canalside architecture found in the maintenance yard, for instance walls rounded so as not to hinder passing wagons, are copied on street corners elsewhere in the town. Another example of a new town associated with the building of a navigation is Ellesmere Port, where the Shropshire Union Canal meets the later Manchester Ship Canal.

Many of the 'inland ports' where navigations meet boasted splendid warehouses built in the straightforward style of the early canals. Shardlow, at the junction of the Trent & Mersey and River Trent, still possesses some fine historic buildings, and others are to be seen at Etruria, Stoke-on-Trent. Those at Banbury and Ellesmere Port are unfortunately no longer in existence, but one can still see fine examples at Leeds and Coventry.

THE SECOND PHASE

It is customary to consider canal architecture as falling into two distinct phases, the earlier being characterised by functional simplicity and an absence of conscious design, the later taking in elements of the neo-classical taste and deliberate ornamentation which arose from the fashionable influence of Grecian architecture as the 18th century reached its close. Canal engineers of the second generation such as Telford, Rennie and Jessop used more advanced techniques made possible by the experience gained with the first canals, creating ambitious cuttings and embankments to give their waterways the shortest possible route across country. The materials used for bridges, aqueducts and buildings in the Brindley age were indigenous: these structures appeared to grow out of the landscape, and the gently blending contour routes could almost have been there by nature rather than by engineering skill. Telford and his contemporaries imposed upon the countryside not only straight routes overcoming obstacles in their path, but monumental structures such as the Lune Aqueduct on the Lancaster Canal and the flight of locks, known as Neptune's Staircase, near Fort William on the Caledonian Canal.

It was the philosophy of the 19th century canal engineers that 'every valley shall be exalted, and every mountain and hill made low' in the service of fast, direct water transport. The technique for doing this has been termed cut and fill. In other words, the material excavated from cuttings was used to build embankments and fill hollows. The result of this pleasing logic can be seen, for instance, on the Grand Union Canal as it crosses the Chilterns or makes its way towards Birmingham via Warwick and Leamington. Instead of the narrow locks of the 18th century canals, the original Bridgewater Canal width limit of 14ft was readopted, permitting the passage of heavily-laden barges carrying nearly twice the capacity of a narrow boat. The wider dimensions, combined with the hitherto unknown engineering ruthlessness of the cut and fill method, created more modern and substantial canals whose character contrasts with those of the 18th century (even though the later canals are still tiny by comparison with British ship canals such as the Gloucester & Sharpness and Caledonian and the enormous continental waterways). The 19th century canals are not only wider, their proportions are different, and locks such as those at Hatton on the Grand Union Canal are on an impressive scale. The encased paddle gear housings repeated on the same canal at Stockton are a feature

Above left to right: Warehouses at Gloucester Dock, Dundas Aqueduct Kennet & Avon Canal, Langley Maltings B.C.N.

opposite: John Rennie's aqueduct carrying the Lancaster Canal over the River Lune near Lancaster

The Hatton flight of 21 locks on the Grand Union Canal near Warwick

The embankment at Burnley, Lancs, carrying the Leeds & Liverpool Canal

Cowley Tunnel Cutting on the Shropshire Union Canal near Norbury

of this flight; dating from the 1930's, their dockland dimensions and treatment in black and white create a visual harmony.

The Leeds & Liverpool Canal crosses the Pennines in a remarkable feat of construction; it is the only one of the trans-Pennine canal routes still in use as a navigation. Features of both architectural phases are present, it having been built at a period when the transition was taking place. The Leeds & Liverpool contour sections curve around steep hillsides, near East Marton covering a distance of about a mile, as the crow flies, in a series of extensive loops which alone permitted the slow but steady passage of heavily laden barges across the mountain range. This waterway is notable for its short, wide locks, accommodating a 62ft barge which carried 45-50 tons. Elements of the early canals co-exist with the magnificent confidence of John Longbotham's Bingley lock staircases, rising 90ft in less than half a mile, and Robert Whitworth's Burnley embankment (built with spoil from the Gannow cutting and tunnel) which dominates the cotton-mill town. Both structures are numbered by enthusiasts among the seven wonders of the waterways. A canal of contrasts, it alternates between industrial towns with superb waterside factories and warehouses, and peaceful moorland countryside. Bridges and cottages are largely of millstone grit, giving it that purposeful, realistic air which characterised the communities it served.

The bridges and aqueducts of the second phase are also impressive. A greater use of cast iron brought a new ornamentation and flexibility of design to bridges. Even where the traditional materials were used, a wider curve and flatter parapet contrasted with the smaller and more arched bridges of the early canals. There are good examples of the later style on the Shropshire Union Canal, and the high bridges, for instance spanning the Woodseaves cutting near Stafford, are remarkable for their lofty construction. The double bridge at Stoke Bruerne illustrates a dignified confidence of line and proportion which contrasts with the endearing near-crudity of some of the very early structures. The sophisticated design at Grove, Watford, was introduced to please the owner of a manorial park adjoining the canal; others, like the river bridge at Stourport, were made imposing by size and ornament to bolster municipal pride. The impressive Old Ferrybridge over the Aire & Calder Navigation near Leeds is inscribed *John Carr Esquire, of York, Architect 1797; Richard Hartley of Pontefract, Builder 1804.*

It was no longer enough for structures to conform to their uses; they had taken on another function, that of consciously beautifying the landscape rather than unobtrusively enhancing it. At the end of the 18th century people looked back to the golden age of classical Greece and Rome; they tried to imitate the bygone culture in many ways, in dress, furniture, poetry and painting. This pervading fashion filtered towards the engineers of the day, influencing their designs and leading them to produce many beautiful objects. Despite the new emphasis on decoration, these structures performed their tasks extremely well. John Rennie, considered by some to have been an even better architect than he was an engineer, adorned the Kennet & Avon Canal in particular with some superb work. Details such as the balustrading on his Dundas aqueduct, not to mention the neo-classical swags and niches of the Sydney Road Tunnel bridge in Bath, confirm his taste and skill.

Tunnels were made wide enough for two boats to pass, and some had towing paths. They were given ornamental portals, such as on the sadly decayed Sapperton near Stroud, Thames & Severn Canal, where much of the castellated parapet has been dislodged. Architectural uniformity was imposed upon the Gloucester & Sharpness Canal, not completed until 1827, so that one attractive classical bridge house design prevailed

The double arched bridge at Stoke Bruerne near Northampton on the Grand Union Canal

The clock tower at Stourport, Staffordshire and Worcestershire Canal

from one end to the other, contrasting with the individual treatment of each cottage on the 18th century canals. At Stourport the former clock warehouse is surmounted by a clock tower of 1812 – a masterpiece of simple but effective design. The clock face itself is worthy of note since it has the old Roman IIII instead of IV, the latter being more common on clock faces after about 1700.

Thomas Telford is justly admired for his lock houses where observation porches and low roofs jutting out over bay windows are to be seen in particular on the Shropshire Union and Caledonian Canals. They show an affinity with contemporary lodges at the entrance to stately homes and turnpike toll houses. William Jessop, from whom Telford learnt a great deal, built a number of similar houses on the Grand Junction Canal. Where the canal is embanked they often deceptively appear to be bungalows, the upper floor being on the level of the canal and containing the office, the lower coinciding with the lane outside.

Many superb industrial buildings date from this period, some of the best stone warehouses being at Sowerby Bridge, West Yorkshire, where the Calder & Hebble Navigation is joined by the Rochdale Canal. Langley Maltings on the Titford Canal, Birmingham, display red brick building at its best, while the extensive and beautiful warehouses at Gloucester stand quietly musing on their past. Gloucester Docks were scheduled as an outstanding conservation area during European Architectural Heritage Year, a well-deserved accolade for an area of great historical and architectural importance. Old prints of the Regent's Canal show how fine were once the warehouses at Paddington Basin and City Road.

The distinction between the two main phases of canal architecture is sometimes blurred, since 19th century canals follow the contours for part of their routes and 18th century canals have examples of deliberate ornamentation, especially in the proximity of stately homes. Some early waterways were subsequently improved. The latter is particularly apparent where later engineers straightened the old meandering Brindley routes. On the north Oxford Canal, William Cubitt was responsible for new bridges of particular grace when he shortened Brindley's winding canal route across country. Similarly, Thomas Telford was engaged to shorten the old Birmingham Canal main line, thereby creating the new main line route. Where his new section bypassed the Brindley loops, decorative cast iron bridges were often made to carry the towing path across the old canal. Some of the loops were retained as lay-bys for loading and mooring, examples being the Hockley Port and Oozells Street loops on the Birmingham Canal. On the Oxford Canal many of the loops served no further purpose and have disappeared, apart from a short stretch spanned by an elegant bridge where they were cut off by the new line. One such loop ran through the disused tunnel by the church at Newbold-on-Avon near Rugby, and the old line can still be traced across the fields.

IRON AND THE VICTORIAN INDUSTRIAL AGE

During the 19th century the use of cast iron as a construction material radically altered the approach to industrial architecture. Before the 18th century people had known how to produce cast iron, but it had mostly been converted to wrought iron by a second process rather than being used in its own right. One of the greatest factors hampering the development of a cast iron industry, and thus its use for building, was the shortage of charcoal, then used in the blast furnaces. Abraham Darby, the first of a line of iron-masters bearing the same name, moved to Coalbrookdale in 1708 and discovered how to use coke in his blast furnaces rather than charcoal, a step which eventually brought about a revolution in the British cast iron industry. Cast iron cooking pots from Coalbrookdale became famous and cast iron came into use for all kinds of domestic objects as well as for engineering construction.

A song published in 1822 made satirical use of the subject.

Since cast-iron has got all the rage,
And scarce anything's now made without it;
As I live in this cast-iron age,
I mean to say something about it.
There's cast-iron coffins and carts.
There's cast-iron bridges and boats.
Corn-factors with cast-iron hearts,
That I'd hang up in cast-iron coats....

So great is the fashion of late
We have cast-iron hammers and axes;
And, if we may judge by their weight,
We have plenty of cast-iron taxes.

this page: The world's first iron bridge over the River Severn in Shropshire

opposite: The Anderton Lift near Northwich in Cheshire. It links the River Weaver to the Trent & Mersey Canal

During the 18th century cast iron was used in mill buildings as a construction material. Already it supported structures in the form of invisible girders and stanchions, but it was becoming increasingly common to exploit the decorative possibilities of the material itself and the canal builders were pioneers in finding new ways of using it.

Pontcysyllte aqueduct carrying the Llangollen Canal across the River Dee in North Wales

Stretton aqueduct carrying the Shropshire Union Canal over Telford's Holyhead road

Telford's aqueduct carrying the Engine Arm of the Birmingham Canal Navigations over his New Main Line

The world's first iron bridge, spanning the Severn near Coalbrookdale and dating from 1781, was contemporary with the 18th century canals. A truly remarkable achievement – the first of its kind but no tentative experiment – the bridge caught the imagination of contemporaries and is still marvelled at today. It was built by Abraham Derby III at a time when his iron-making complex was the largest single such concern in Britain. The high span was made necessary by the many sailing barges which traded on the river at that time. The choice of iron rather than timber or stone was vindicated when the bridge survived a great flood in February 1795. *It firmly stood and dauntless braved the storm* while every other bridge over the Severn was severely damaged. No doubt this triumph contributed to the increasing use of iron in the next century. The project proved fairly expensive; as a result it was several decades before bridges made entirely of cast iron came into more general use.

Iron was employed particularly in the field of transport, and Telford used it for road and canal bridges. Many of these have survived on the canals whereas they have been removed from the roads. His cast iron trough aqueduct on the Shrewsbury Canal at Longdon-on-Tern, like the Iron Bridge, was constructed in the heart of the Shropshire cast iron country. It was box-like and supported by struts. Likewise, many of the first cast iron structures on the existing canal system were strictly functional. The highly regarded Pontcysyllte (1805) and Chirk aqueducts attributed to Telford impress by the way they dominate the landscape rather than because of any superficial ornamentation, which would in any case be rendered incongruous by their sheer size. A light, ethereal quality was achieved by making the iron trough itself watertight, dispensing with a ponderous all-masonry structure filled with puddled clay. Much of the cast iron for the Llangollen Canal came from the Plas Kynaston works nearby. The aqueducts consist of cast iron sections bolted together and this, rather than the dovetailed joints and wedges of the Iron Bridge, became the most common form of construction. Stone piers support the trough, which at Chirk is encased in masonry; at Pontcysyllte the towing path is cantilevered out over the water channel, whereas at Chirk it is of solid masonry on the outside of the trough. Edstone, a slightly later aqueduct on the Stratford-upon-Avon Canal, copies Telford's experimental aqueduct at Longdon-on-Tern by having the towing path slung alongside the water, so that when walking over it one's eyes are at water level. There are many iron trough bridges, whose square-cut design moves away from the naive semicircular arch of earlier brick or stone equivalents.

The aqueduct at Stretton, on the Shropshire Union Canal, dated 1832 and also designed by Telford, has a certain ornamental character created by the use of square panels and a supporting arch – now attractively picked out in white – with curved stone piers. The charmingly patterned handrail is reminiscent of those which enhance the footbridges on the Widcombe flight of the Kennet & Avon Canal in Bath. The aqueduct, although basically similar to the iron troughs already described, gives the first hint of the decorative style which reached its greatest height on the Birmingham Canal Navigations, where Telford created such ecclesiastical masterpieces as the Engine Arm Aqueduct over his new main line at Smethwick. Rows of gothic arches and impeccable details rival any Victorian rood- or organ-screen.

Equally beautiful, if less elaborate in design, are the bridges once cast at the Horseley Ironworks. They consist of sections bolted together, with a continuous handrail cast in four pieces. Widely used, especially in the Midlands, these graceful spans are to be seen at Spon Lane near Farmer's Bridge, Birmingham, at Braunston near Rugby and many other places. They represent the freedom of cast iron prefabrication, being neither crude in construction nor unnecessarily ornate. The lightness was permitted by the fact that, being towing path bridges, they needed to carry neither water nor vehicles. Telford's road bridge at Holt Fleet over the Severn is, however, elegant in design although extremely strong. Far heavier in appearance is Macclesfield (or *Blow-up*) Bridge over the Regent's Canal in London, whose massive columns were provided by the Coalbrookdale company in 1820. Here the principle of the Telford aqueducts and Horseley bridges is reversed, for masonry arches designed to bear heavy traffic are supported by iron piers. The latter survived a petroleum and gunpowder explosion in 1874, testifying to their durability.

Although boat lifts were able to accomplish a change of level more quickly than a flight of locks and were once quite common, of the inclined planes and vertical lifts once in use in this country there is now only one working example – at Anderton near Northwich in Cheshire. The great lifts on defunct waterways such as the Ketley and Bude ran into operational problems and were abandoned along with the canals.

The Anderton Lift is a monument to the lasting qualities of cast and wrought iron. Built in 1875 and converted from a hydraulic mechanism to electricity in 1906-7, it is still in full working order despite suffering extensive corrosion which was made good during 1974-5. It raises boats vertically in two caissons or troughs through 50 feet from the River Weaver to an aqueduct leading to the Trent & Mersey Canal. Before its construction, goods had to be transhipped at this point; engineer Edward Leader Williams recommended to the Weaver Trust that a vertical lift would be quicker than a flight of locks and would take no water from the canal, this being the chief disadvantage of a lock connection between the two waterways.

The lift was built on an island in the river, thus necessitating a linking aqueduct to the Trent & Mersey, made of wrought (not cast) iron. Also of wrought iron, the troughs measure 75 feet long by 15 feet 6 inches wide. When filled with water they originally counterbalanced each other, but, following the conversion to electricity in 1906-7, cast iron weights working over new pulleys at the top were added to counterbalance the weight of the troughs. The enormous girders, buttresses and pulleys combined to create a gigantic effect, now somewhat diminished by the industrial buildings on the other side of the river. But to see it at work makes one respect the power and majesty of iron and to understand the almost religious confidence it gave to 19th century structural design.

The cast-iron bridge at Smethwick, over the Birmingham Canal Navigations

A Horseley Ironworks bridge on the north Oxford Canal near Rugby

Macclesfield Bridge over the Regent's Canal near London Zoo

Peter Bartle April '75.

THE WORKING ENVIRONMENT

The canal companies created groups of waterside buildings from which their activities were carried out. These buildings have a particular character derived from the bringing together of all the individual functions essential to the upkeep and running of the waterways. These groups must be preserved intact as a living environment which brings history alive, for to many people an important ingredient of the canal experience is the echo from our commercial past held fast in bricks and mortar. Communities, as opposed to the individual lock or bridge house, are usually found at canal junctions or termini. Workshops, offices, pubs, stores – all make their contribution to an architectural unity.

Canalside warehouses and storage buildings contained a diverse selection of commodities. Those at Ellesmere Wharf on the Llangollen Canal housed big round cheeses when Cheshire cheese was produced alongside the canal and conveyed by boat. Timber, which still plays an important part in canal freight traffic on the commercial waterways, was stored both for transport elsewhere and for use in canal maintenance. Bales of raw cotton destined for the Lancashire mills and coal intended for industry or for use in the company offices, workshops and cottages contributed to the busy community of a canalside yard in simple brick-built sheds or impressive warehouses.

Stables were essential to canal yards, not only for the horses on which company clerks, surveyors and foremen inspected the waterways, but for the boat horses and donkeys which were the means of propulsion for canal craft. Here the beasts were rested, fed and watered between one long haul and another, while loading or unloading took place. Often now used for storage or workshops, the buildings are easily recognisable by their one-storey construction and numerous doors. Stables were common not only in yards, but at flights of locks (for instance at Bunbury on the Shropshire Union Canal) or at the end of a tunnel. This was a natural halting point for the horse since he would be led on a track over the hill, arriving before the boat, which would be laboriously *legged* through.

Boat repairs were an important activity at some yards, which had a covered dry or wet dock, usually for routine work on canal maintenance craft. No doubt emergency repairs were undertaken on commercial boats to enable them to reach one of the independent boat

opposite: The former water tower at Bulbourne maintenance yard on the Grand Union Canal near Tring

builders. Most dry docks are in simple brick buildings, some with louvred windows, as at Marsworth on the Grand Union Canal. Carpenters' and blacksmiths' shops are often found at maintenance yards.

Canal wharves were usually cobbled, or paved with brick or granite setts, these being the traditional surfaces for areas where goods were loaded and unloaded. Semi-circular heel grips were placed under lock gate balance beams. Elegant cranes are sometimes still in position, although the horses, wheelbarrows and sacks are there no longer. Still present, though, are many of the mooring rings and bollards to which the boats were tied alongside the hard wharf edge, where deep water was created to accommodate many boats. Bulls Bridge, Southall, where the Grand Junction Canal and Paddington Arm join, was once famous for the number of narrow boats which could be seen there.

The blacksmith's shop at Bulbourne maintenance yard on the Grand Union Canal at Tring

Canal workers' cottages and waterside factories, although disparate in function, were constructed on the same general principles and in a group they blend for a number of reasons. Cottages, factories and other buildings were made at the same period and of the same materials – locally-burnt brick or locally-quarried stone – giving an effect of unity and belonging which intensifies the family nature of these groups. Sometimes a mill was one of the elements of a group, as at Cheddleton on the Caldon Canal where a flint mill and a silk mill in close proximity to the fine old cottages are together in harmony with the landscape. In an urban context, at Etruria, where the same canal joins its parent Trent & Mersey the historic bone and flint mill is still to be seen.

The Etruscan Bone and Flint Mill at the junction of the Trent & Mersey Canal and its Caldon Branch

It is a continuing source of surprise and pleasure to the canal traveller to see how architectural groups with a workaday function were beautified by simple, dignified touches. At Bulbourne on the Grand Union Canal the workshops, although mundane in themselves, are splendidly surmounted by an italianate tower and are enhanced by some beautiful windows made large enough to shed light on the work being done within. The semi-circular fanlight over the main door is a true gem and there are some fine associated dwellings, especially the house constructed for the manager at the north end of the site.

Pumping houses built to accommodate steam engines are normally plain in appearance. Those at Crofton and Claverton, on the Kennet & Avon Canal, are architecturally unpretentious but inside one cannot fail to be impressed by the magnificence of the beam mechanism at Crofton, and the power of Claverton's great undershot waterwheels which lift the water bodily from the river Avon. Tringford pumping station on the Wendover Arm of the Grand Union Canal is a more imposing building and like Bulbourne it has elegant semi-circular arched windows. Here water is pumped from four reservoirs to the Marsworth summit of the canal, a task which was once performed by beam engines similar to those at Crofton. They have now been replaced by electric motors.

The interior of the pumping station on the Kennet & Avon Canal at Claverton near Bath

Pumping stations were sometimes placed at junctions to prevent one canal company's water flowing into an adjoining canal. More often they were strategically placed at either side of a canal summit, to maintain water levels by pumping the water back to the top of a flight of locks, or to pump water into the canal from an adjacent reservoir, as at Braunston. Canal junctions are often enhanced by elegant houses such as those at Fazeley (where the Coventry Canal meets the Birmingham & Fazeley) and at King's Norton, the junction of the Worcester & Birmingham and the Stratford-upon-Avon Canals. They preside over the passing boats with greater architectural pretension than the cottages found elsewhere on the four canals.

Toll houses are sometimes still found amongst

The maintenance yard at Hartshill on the Coventry Canal near Nuneaton

The Holly Bush at Denford on the Caldon Canal near Stoke-on-Trent

The Admiral Nelson at Braunston on the Grand Union Canal near Daventry

groups of buildings and also at stopping places along the canals such as flights of locks. One of the best known examples is the recently restored octagonal toll house at Bratch on the Staffordshire & Worcestershire Canal. Elevated above the road, its pitched roof and 18th century windows impart a distinctive individuality to the area. Many more toll houses were once to be found on the canal system, but their form was so closely allied to their original purpose that when tolls ceased to be paid they became obsolete. It was difficult to adapt them to new functions and many disappeared. A few are still in existence, for example at Walsall, West Midlands, and at Stourport where one has been turned into a little shop. Their design was largely adopted from the turnpike roads. A characteristic plan and abundance of windows (for that period) allowed a good view of approaching traffic on the road or canal. Something not unlike a toll house plan was used by Telford for lock cottages, notably on the Shropshire Union, whose viewing porches performed the same function. Immediate recognition was one of the advantages of the unmistakable toll house design.

The roofs of canal company premises were sometimes dignified by the addition of a clock and bell tower. There are fine examples at Northwich on the Weaver Navigation and at Hartshill on the Coventry Canal. The towers performed an essential task, for the clocks would chime the hour, telling the canal workers when to begin and when to finish work in an age when the wristwatch was unknown, and the fob watch was the prerogative of the middle class.

Waterside pubs, provided for the refreshment of the boat people, were often specially built, although some pre-date the canals. With the decline of narrow boat traffic, many had to turn their backs to the canal and cultivate the road-user's custom, although they were still architecturally orientated towards the water – the means by which their original customers had arrived. Pubs were the gathering places of the boat people and many landlords flattered their clientèle by adopting names such as the Navigation, the Boat, the Grand Junction, the Duke of Bridgewater or even the Jolly Boatman. As buildings, many are indistinguishable from contemporary local houses or cottages and exhibit similar features, such as foursquare brick construction (often whitewashed) with small windows and high pitched roofs. The Admiral Nelson at Braunston on the Grand Union Canal still retains the appearance of a quiet, self-effacing country pub devoted to a small community of customers who arrived by water every so often at the beginning or end of a commercial run, or while their boats were laid up for repairs. The Globe Inn at Linslade, also on the Grand Union Canal, is completely water-orientated and this forms part of its appeal even to land travellers. The Black Lion at Consall Forge on the Caldon Canal is best approached by water and occupies an unrivalled position on the hill beside this little-known waterway.

The Navigation at Barrow-on-Soar, which attracted the attention of L. T. C. Rolt (related in *Narrow Boat*), is a characteristically simple building beside a hump-backed bridge, creating the harmony of square and curved shapes which is so pleasing to the eye and inviting to the thirsty canal traveller.

Where the dignity of the canal company dictated greater pomp and circumstance, canalside public houses were grander in appearance. Such is the Tontine Hotel at Stourport, which faces the River Severn where it meets the Staffordshire & Worcestershire Canal. This was a residential hotel for people who came to trade when Stourport was one of the busiest canal centres; its Georgian facade and grandiose entrance hall speak of its former commercial importance.

FROM CONSTRUCTION TO CONSERVATION

In general, the buildings did not form a large part of the capital cost of canal construction. Buying of land, excavation, earth moving, walling and bank work were some of the most expensive items. Shortage of funds led to simplicity in architecture. Anything elaborate and therefore costly was reserved for canal company headquarters, or confined to decorative details. Indeed, the Telford masterpieces at Chirk and Pontcysyllte were given iron tanks partly to avoid the prohibitive expense of massive stone or brick structures.

Although money was scarce at the time most canals were built by local groups of landowners and industrialists, it usually flowed in from investors in other parts of the country when trade began to flourish. Many canals were profitable: for instance, it is estimated that in 1829 the Loughborough Navigation, Mersey & Irwell, Trent & Mersey, Birmingham, Oxford, Erewash and Coventry Canals paid dividends from 36% to 140%; and some were still paying over 30% in 1838. Waterway shares acquired a get-rich-quick reputation. Impractical canal schemes, entered into purely for financial gain, were among the first to decline. Never completed, they were abandoned in favour of a new speculative venture: the railways.

From the first, canals were supplemented by land-based transport. Wagonways, plateways, tramways with rails of wood, stone or iron: these were known and used in collieries and in iron works such as Coalbrookdale 50 years before the age of canal building. Inclined planes, too, with water-filled caissons running on rails, co-existed with canals. Many of the Welsh canals could not have operated successfully without tramways which covered ground inaccessible by water. The Cromford & High Peak Railway, built in 1830, connected the Cromford Canal to the Peak Forest Canal at Whaley Bridge. Some independent railways were built, starting with the Stockton & Darlington, completed in 1825; construction gathered momentum in the 1830's. Sometimes the canals carried materials for building railways and some canal beds served as the basis for railways, such as the Uttoxeter branch of the Caldon Canal. The existing tunnel on the Thames & Medway Canal was used by the

opposite:
The former inclined plane at Foxton on the Leicester section of the Grand Union Canal near Market Harborough

above: The Almond Aqueduct on the Union Canal in Scotland.

Hazlehurst Aqueduct carrying the Leek Branch of the Caldon Canal over the main line, not far from Stoke-on-Trent

new railway, and for a time both boats and trains passed through it. Waterways supplied the potential for their own decline by contributing a great deal of engineering knowledge, particularly about building embankments and cuttings, and by conveying materials required to create the new railway system. In early railway construction, bridges and viaducts were almost identical in design to those on the 19th century canals. Indeed, certain canal engineers were commissioned by the emerging railway companies.

Railways' obvious advantages, such as their speed and flexibility, did not perhaps weigh as strongly with those who backed them as did the grand idea of railways – in tune with the Victorian age – and of a new investment which might be as profitable as the previous one. With this in mind, from the mid-1840's a number of canal companies turned to building railways or allowed themselves to be bought by railway companies (such extensive railway ownership of most of Britain's canals resulted in their nationalisation along with the railways in 1948). The canals soon lost their passenger traffic to the new trains but freight was unaffected for a time. Growing competition later forced the canals to reduce their tolls and resulted in heavy losses of revenue.

Throughout the late 19th and early 20th centuries some of the railway/canal companies resorted to tactics such as raising canal tolls, deliberately neglecting maintenance and creating delays for the boatmen in order to compel freight to be transferred from the canals to the railways. It is indicative of the canals' commercial success that such artificial means had to be employed. Canals still carried 13 million tons in 1938. High charges and a lack of co-ordination between companies meant that even though canals such as the Grand Union or the railway-controlled Birmingham network flourished well into the present century, most had succumbed by the Second World War or earlier. The motorised narrow boat could go almost anywhere on the main system apart from the Leeds & Liverpool Canal, but the bigger and more efficient barges were debarred by their size from the smaller-gauge canals. In the 1930's the Grand Union was improved from London to Birmingham to take the bigger craft. Even today, however, there are commercial niches in our economy for canals and railways as well as motorways. All can exist in a complementary fashion. The present cost of fuel suggests that the most economical of these systems, waterways, should be fully utilised.

Nationalisation of most of the waterways took place in 1948. The system was based on that controlled by the Minister of War Transport during the Second World War. Notable exceptions were the Thames, Manchester Ship Canal and the Bridgewater Canal, Great Ouse, Nene, Yorkshire Ouse and the Broads. Some already abandoned navigations were also excluded, such as the Basingstoke and Thames & Severn Canals. The nationalised waterways about 2,000 miles of them, passed to the newly created British Waterways Board on the abolition of the British Transport Commission in 1962.

The canalised rivers of the north east (the Aire & Calder, River Trent, Sheffield & South Yorkshire Navigations), plus the River Weaver, which joins the Mersey estuary, and the Gloucester & Sharpness Canal in the south west, carried, and still continue to carry, appreciable tonnages each year, consisting mainly of coal, oil, timber and general merchandise.

The Transport Act of 1968 classified the Board's waterways as commercial (roughly a fifth) and cruising (just over half), leaving the remainder, of which a number were derelict. The Board were to deal with the remainder waterways in the most economical manner possible, consistent with the requirements of public health and the preservation of amenity and safety, but the Act empowered local authorities to make funds available to restore them for leisure purposes. These waterways contained some of the most impressive structures and buildings of the system, for instance the Marple and Hazlehurst aqueducts and the flight of locks at Devizes, on the Peak Forest, Caldon and Kennet & Avon Canals respectively. Canal enthusiasts had already identified the existence of such priceless items and regretted the passing of those which had already been lost when their original use expired, such as toll houses. The 1968 Act made it possible for the cost of restoration and improvement to be shared between the Board, local authorities and volunteers, who also provided labour to supplement the work of the Board's engineering staff. Under these arrangements the Board usually contribute the sum they would have needed to spend to make the canal meet the requirements of a remainder waterway. Many local authorities, for instance Greater Manchester and Stoke-on-Trent, have come to the admirable decision that money is well spent to enable pleasure cruising and other leisure activities to take place on waterways.

The flight of locks at Ancoats, Manchester, on the Ashton Canal

Stretches of canal are being designated by local authorities as part of conservation areas, and the Board welcome the adoption of towing paths by local authorities as public walks, especially through towns. The Board welcome voluntary work too, provided it is organised by responsible societies working in close collaboration with the Board's staff, and they appreciate the co-operation of trades unions in agreeing to the use of volunteers for canal restoration. It is the Board's policy, although their resources are not sufficient for their tasks, to retain and restore buildings wherever possible for their visual qualities and historical associations. If the original function is obsolete, new water-related uses can be found for them.

The towing path walk beside the Regent's Canal adopted by the London Borough of Camden

The Montgomery Canal provides an example of co-operation achieving the restoration of a derelict stretch of remainder waterway. It is a branch of the Shropshire Union system, running 30 miles from Frankton Junction on the Llangollen Canal via Welshpool. Completed to Newtown in 1821, it enabled timber and limestone to be carried away from Montgomeryshire (now Powys) and coal and grain to be brought to the towns and villages along the route. The canal was breached just south of Frankton in 1936, cutting off the connection with the main line. Never repaired, the canal became derelict and it was abandoned in 1944. Commercial traffic had ceased by the end of the 1930's and no one foresaw the influx of pleasure boats, which in the 1970's were to clog the Llangollen Canal in summer, largely because of the fame of its two aqueducts.

In 1971 the Board's Amenity Services Division produced a comprehensive amenity study, in consultation with other interested bodies, demonstrating the variety of leisure activities which could be introduced even should the canal not be fully restored, for example fishing and fish rearing, canoeing, camping and picnicking. For those interested in the architectural history of the waterways, there are three fine aqueducts of considerable interest, including the one over the River Vyrnwy near Llanymynech.

Welshpool Borough Council obtained from the Department of the Environment a grant of £10,000 to which they added £2,000 of their own for improving the canal within the borough boundary. Clearance work was undertaken by members of the Shropshire Union Canal Society and in October 1973 came the news that the Prince of Wales Committee were prepared to give their support to restoring to full amenity standards the seven-mile stretch from Welshpool to Arddleen as part of their work to improve the environment in Wales. In May 1974, 30 years after abandonment, Welshpool Town Lock was officially re-opened by the Prince of Wales. The restoration of the first seven miles may be only a beginning; the rest of the canal may follow.

The Vyrnwy aqueduct on the Montgomery Canal at Carreghofa near Oswestry

THE PROPOSED SCHEME AT WIGAN PIER ON THE LEEDS & LIVERPOOL CANAL

RESURRECTION

The restoration of derelict waterways was a question which entered few minds at the end of the inter-war period. After all, what purpose did they serve? They had been built for freight traffic, which had disappeared except from a number of broad, commercially-viable waterways and a very few narrow canals. Pleasure boats, although they had always existed, were few.

After the second World War interest in pleasure cruising grew. In 1944 L.T.C. Rolt published *Narrow Boat*. This story of a journey in a converted traditional craft has stimulated much enthusiasm, then and since. Canal cruising clubs were formed and there was a steady increase in the numbers of privately owned boats and hire cruiser bases. The architect and photographer Eric de Maré showed in his books a great appreciation of the visual qualities of canal buildings and urged their preservation as part of our heritage. He pointed out their vital nature: for, being part and parcel of the canal experience, their removal could only detract from the value of that experience and make our country the poorer.

So it was, in the post-war years, that a new approach came about which saw the canals not merely in the light of their commercial viability but with some of the romantic glow that now surrounds the steam railways in the eyes of the devotees. The effect of time on structures has mellowed them and invested them with a hallowed aura of age; which is not to denigrate their intrinsic worth and beauty. Steps worn away by countless boatmen's feet; bridge guards toothed by towing ropes rubbing away for so long that they have gone through the cast iron almost as if it were cheese. A patina of lichens enhances an old roof or bridge; it does not detract. This has to be borne in mind when maintenance is being carried out. The right choice of colours can blend in new buildings and reveal the essential qualities of the old. Everywhere the atmosphere of the past, which brings pleasure and satisfaction to casual users and to canal enthusiasts alike, can be fostered.

The new interest in industrial archaeology and the growing appreciation by ordinary people of Britain's architectural heritage, stimulated by European Architectural Heritage Year 1975, are helping to put the waterways in their rightful place and securing their recognition as important elements in the architectural and industrial history of Britain in the last two centuries.

opposite: The flight of locks at Marple on the Peak Forest Canal near Stockport, Cheshire

The proposed scheme at Etruria, Stoke-on-Trent, on the Caldon Canal

Sketch showing how old canalside buildings can be rehabilitated to accommodate new water related uses

Wardle lock house on the Trent & Mersey Canal at Middlewich

Bingley Five Rise locks on the Leeds & Liverpool Canal near Bradford

The maintenance yard at Northwich, Cheshire, on the Weaver Navigation

The 1968 Transport Act gave government blessing to the new approach and encouraged public enjoyment of the canals and rivers, while acknowledging that freight carrying was the right use for those waterways where it could flourish in present-day conditions. The Board were charged with maintaining more than half of their waterways for the leisure of ordinary people. It was realised that the future value of structures such as cottages and warehouses associated with the waterways would need special consideration, so an Architect/Planner was appointed.

Since 1970 his work has been largely concerned with the rehabilitation of the canal fabric, locks, maintenance yards and individual buildings and structures as well as major schemes for the development of local authority or private land alongside the canals. Staff of the Board are now guided in the important task of making old buildings and structures pleasing to the eye as well as performing a job of work. The Board's Waterway Environment Handbook (1972) has been widely circulated, to all local authorities through whose areas the Board's canals and rivers run, and to other interested bodies such as universities, planning consultancies and canal societies. It contains a series of advisory case studies showing ways of renovating waterside locations such as locks in urban and rural settings, and how basins, lay-bys and boating stations can be designed. Advice ranges from the general – the broad layout and appearance of these areas including paint colours and surfacing – to the particular: the individual treatment of details such as bollards, seats and trees.

A number of sites have won Civic Trust awards, for example the James Brindley Walk scheme at Cambrian Wharf undertaken in association with Birmingham Corporation, and the London Borough of Camden's Towing Path Walk. Others have won commendations. In 1975 the Board gained a special heritage year award for continuing contributions to conservation and other awards for their canal improvement schemes. These recognised the Board's work in re-opening for navigation and recreation the Ashton Canal from Ducie Street, Manchester to Dukinfield Junction, Ashton-under-Lyne; at Bingley, near Bradford, enhancing the spectacular Five-Rise locks and their surroundings; and in Cheshire improving Middlewich Wharf and Red Bull Yard on the Trent & Mersey Canal, Northwich Yard on the River Weaver Navigation, and repairing the Anderton Lift which links these waterways.

In addition, structural repair of Great Haywood Bridge in Staffordshire, repair and redecoration of locks, cottages and the aqueduct at Hazlehurst Junction on the Caldon Canal in Staffordshire, and the repair and rehabilitation of the locks at Bratch, Wombourne, in Staffordshire were commended by the Civic Trust, while not earning awards.

Commenting on the Board's programme of visual improvements to the canal system, the Civic Trust said that schemes such as these were beginning to make a significant difference to the appearance of the canal scene in all parts of the country.

This programme includes restoration of complete waterways with local authority help, rehabilitation of ancient monuments, facelifting maintenance yards and adapting old commercial waterside buildings for new purposes connected with the leisure use of waterways.

Maintenance yards often have unusual architectural features. They are still busy areas concerned with the upkeep of the waterways. The group of slate-roofed red and brindle brick waterside buildings at Hartshill was the distinctive headquarters of the old Coventry Canal Company and is particularly interesting because it includes the elegant dock building with its bell-tower and clock. The tower was restored together with replace-

The Ashton Canal at Dukinfield near Manchester

The Hazlehurst flight of locks on the Caldon Canal near Stoke-on-Trent

Brindley's bridge at Great Haywood, where the Trent & Mersey joins the Staffordshire & Worcestershire Canal, before returfing

ments and repairs to windows and roofs, and overall external decoration. Screening, surfacing and modest landscaping resulted in the working spaces becoming more efficient. The house and certain canal cottages were redecorated to achieve a comprehensive treatment.

In 1972 it was decided to move the Board's hire cruiser base from Oxford to Hillmorton, near Rugby, where the Oxford Canal Company had their major workshops and dry docks. The scheme involved adapting a once busy commercial centre with a lay-by arm, dry dock, stores, workplaces and blacksmith's shop to the needs of leisure boating. Several of the former engineers' stores and sheds were converted to provide accommodation for the fleet superintendent. External decoration, reconstruction of the bell tower, roof repairs and new doors and windows were in sympathy with the small scale and historical associations of the area, while surfacing, screen fencing and a minor landscape scheme improved the canalside.

Red Bull Yard, near the junction of the Macclesfield and Trent & Mersey Canals, was originally an engineering administrative and maintenance centre. Recently it was returned to this use by the Board when a tenancy expired. The opportunity was taken not only to convert the old buildings to accommodate engineering staff, but also to improve and tidy neglected structures and the wharf areas. With a public house nearby on the Congleton Road, the wharf and its environs are an attractive stopping-place for boats cruising on the Trent & Mersey Canal or intending to cruise on the Macclesfield Canal from Hardingswood Junction.

Where an ancient monument was involved, at Great Haywood near Stafford, the Board achieved a really authentic restoration. The junction bridge where the Trent & Mersey and Staffordshire & Worcestershire Canals meet is listed as being of historical interest and is one of the best examples of James Brindley's work. The scheme, which included strengthening the 9 inch brick ring arch, stabilising the soffit and rebuilding the arch spandrels, was enhanced by sandblasting and pointing to match the tone of the original lime mortar. The deck was relaid, brick paving revealed and restored to produce an attractive context in which the elegant proportions of the bridge itself could be appreciated.

The 1968 Transport Act paved the way for the restoration of a significant number of derelict waterways in the next seven years. The Ashton and lower Peak Forest Canals near Manchester represent one of the most extreme examples of rescue from deterioration that have occurred so far on the Board's system. The waterside mills, factories and warehouses which still remain speak eloquently of their once busy commercial past. Although freight traffic declined between the wars, it continued until a disastrous fire in 1954 destroyed a mill which had received coal via the two canals. Situated in a vandal-prone industrial area, the Ashton Canal soon became clogged with rubbish and unsafe from lack of maintenance after the disappearance of commercial boats. In the early 1960's, when vandalism at the Manchester end of the Ashton Canal was at its height, the water in the aqueduct at Store Street was piped to deal with leakage which was affecting the road below. On the lower Peak Forest Canal, whose summit pound is the highest on the cruising waterway system, the locks and aqueduct at Marple rapidly deteriorated in the absence of regular traffic and maintenance. The water had to be piped across the aqueduct after a collapse of part of its side. It was scheduled as an ancient monument, on the initiative of Bredbury and Romiley UDC who contributed towards its restoration.

With the help of all the riparian local authorities both canals were restored and re-opened in 1974. Co-operation was established with several industrial and other users having premises alongside the canal, for instance the Anchor Chemical Company carried out a landscaping scheme alongside their factory so workers can sit out and enjoy the sight of boats passing. Nearby, Ancoats Hospital facelifted their canal frontage. The Board believe, and this has been borne out by events so far, that a waterway which has the appearance of being used, on which care and trouble have been spent, is less likely to be vandalised than a derelict, unloved one.

The attractions of a waterside setting both to the boating fraternity and to visitors by land are now being appreciated. At Bathampton on the Kennet & Avon Canal the George has reopened its towing path entrance, and the Royal Cricketers in East London has a new waterside bar made in the former cellars. In various parts of the country there are plans to build new purpose-designed waterside pubs. The first of these was the Long Boat at Cambrian Wharf on the Birmingham & Fazeley Canal, which incorporated a number of traditional features including the use of blue engineering brick, while not trying to conceal its modernity. Its popularity with Birmingham residents and city workers shows the wisdom of the chosen site and design. Many older canalside pubs are attempting to recreate a 'traditional' atmosphere, but in several the new interior decor relies too heavily on the proliferation of rose and castle motifs, which to the narrow boat people would have seemed out of place in a public house. The spartan interior of the Greyhound at Hawkesbury Junction, where the Coventry and Oxford Canals meet, was an example of the surroundings the boat people knew. Many who cared for the simplicity within the canalside pubs mourn its disappearance and regret the vanishing beer engines and the unpressurised beverage they served. Some pubs do remain unspoilt and their owners are becoming aware that this is half their charm. Long may they survive.

For the future, the Board are promoting well-designed waterside schemes which can breathe life into old, abandoned surroundings by adapting canal buildings to provide for increasing recreational demands. For instance, at Etruria in the heart of the Potteries, a comprehensive municipal development centres on the recently restored Caldon Canal where it drops down 19 feet by two locks to join the main line of the Trent & Mersey Canal. The scheme also involves the Etruscan Bone and Flint Mill which has many historic associations. Housing, leisure areas and further landscaping treatment of the canal are included.

At places like Brighouse, on the Calder & Hebble Navigation, and Wigan, Leeds & Liverpool Canal, proposals to rediscover the forgotten canal will create a new focus for the town and an exciting venue for the community. The old buildings will be combined with new to cater for a range of activities and functions. More ambitious schemes at towns like Manchester will demonstrate the social and environmental impact of water areas in urban living. They are designed to make the canal used and enjoyed instead of being a neglected dumping ground for rubbish. In promoting new schemes, as well as restoring individual structures, the Board are acting in accordance with their role as custodians of a living heritage, finding new functions for buildings whose commercial use has disappeared, helping to foster people's enjoyment and appreciation of our legacy from the industrial past.

The Greyhound at Hawkesbury, near Coventry, where the Oxford and Coventry Canals meet

The Royal Cricketers at Old Ford, East London, on the Regent's Canal

The Long Boat at Farmer's Bridge, Birmingham

ILLUSTRATIONS

BIBLIOGRAPHY

The Functional Tradition, J. M. Richards with photographs by Eric de Maré *(Architectural Press 1958)*

The Canals of England, Eric de Maré *(Architectural Press 1950—out of print)*

The Canal Builders, Anthony Burton *(Eyre Methuen 1972)*

Canals and their Architecture, Robert Harris *(Hugh Evelyn 1969)*

Remains of a Revolution, Anthony Burton *(André Deutsch 1975)*

The Archaeology of the Industrial Revolution, Brian Bracegirdle *(Heinemann 1973)*

Waterway Environment Handbook, Peter White *(British Waterways Board) available from Architect/Planner, BWB, The Locks, Hillmorton, Rugby CV21 4PP at £2·30 by post.*

FURTHER READING

Thomas Telford, Brian Bracegirdle and Patricia H. Miles *(David and Charles 1973)*

James Brindley, Engineer 1716–1772, Cyril T. G. Boucher *(Goose and Son 1975)*

ACKNOWLEDGEMENTS

photography by:
Derek Pratt
Leslie Bryce
David Stone
Clay Perry

Line drawings on pages 4, 5, 6, 7, 11, 21, 24, and 37 by **Peter Bartle**

Illustration on page 6 by **Maggie Pryke**

Illustration on page 12 "Marple Aqueduct 1863" courtesy of **Manchester Public Libraries Local History Archive**

Illustration on page 14 "The Northern Entrance to Harecastle Tunnel" courtesy of the **Ronan Picture Library**

Poem on page 21 quoted by permission of **Penguin Books Ltd,** from 'A Touch on the Times' ed. **Roy Palmer 1974**

British Waterways Board, Melbury House, Melbury Terrace, London NW1 6JX

John Ruskin said, "When we build, let us think that we build for ever." The canal engineers of the 18th and 19th centuries built for posterity. Their work was directed not towards the recreation of mankind – for leisure itself was confined to the upper classes – but towards the commercial wealth of the nation and the glorification of the age. Let us not forget their labours; and let us not destroy the beauty they created.

opposite: Cheddleton Mill on the Caldon Canal near Stoke-on-Trent

this page: The High Bridge over the Shropshire Union Canal in Woodseaves Cutting near Stafford